**To all my weird and wonderful friends,
I love you all very much. x**

First published in Great Britain 2021 by Red Shed, part of Farshore

An imprint of HarperCollins*Publishers*
1 London Bridge Street, London SE1 9GF

www.farshore.co.uk

HarperCollins*Publishers*
1st Floor, Watermarque Building, Ringsend Road
Dublin 4, Ireland

Text and illustrations copyright © Sophy Henn 2021

Sophy Henn has asserted her moral rights.

ISBN 978 1 4052 9948 0
Printed in China.
1

Consultancy by Paul Lawston.

A CIP catalogue record for this title is available from the British Library.

# ALL KINDS OF FRIENDS

*Sophy Henn*

RED
SHED

# All kinds of people are friends in all kinds of ways.

Each friendship is very special . . .

. . . but no two are quite the same.

**It's the same for animal friendships too.**

**Some friends go on adventures together.**

Hermit crabs give sea anemones a free ride on their shells. In return, the anemone uses its stinging tentacles to keep octopuses and other predators away.

Friends can look out for you.

Grey langur monkeys sit high up in the trees and use their excellent eyesight to spot predators. Then they warn the chital deer in the forest below when an animal is approaching. WATCH OUT!

Some friends work well together.

Zebras have an excellent sense of smell and ostriches have excellent eyesight, so they combine their skills to stay safe from lions and other predators!

Now and again friends can help
you look your best.

Oxpecker birds catch an easy meal by eating the ticks and parasites on hippos' bodies. YUMMY! This helps keep the hippos looking spick and span.

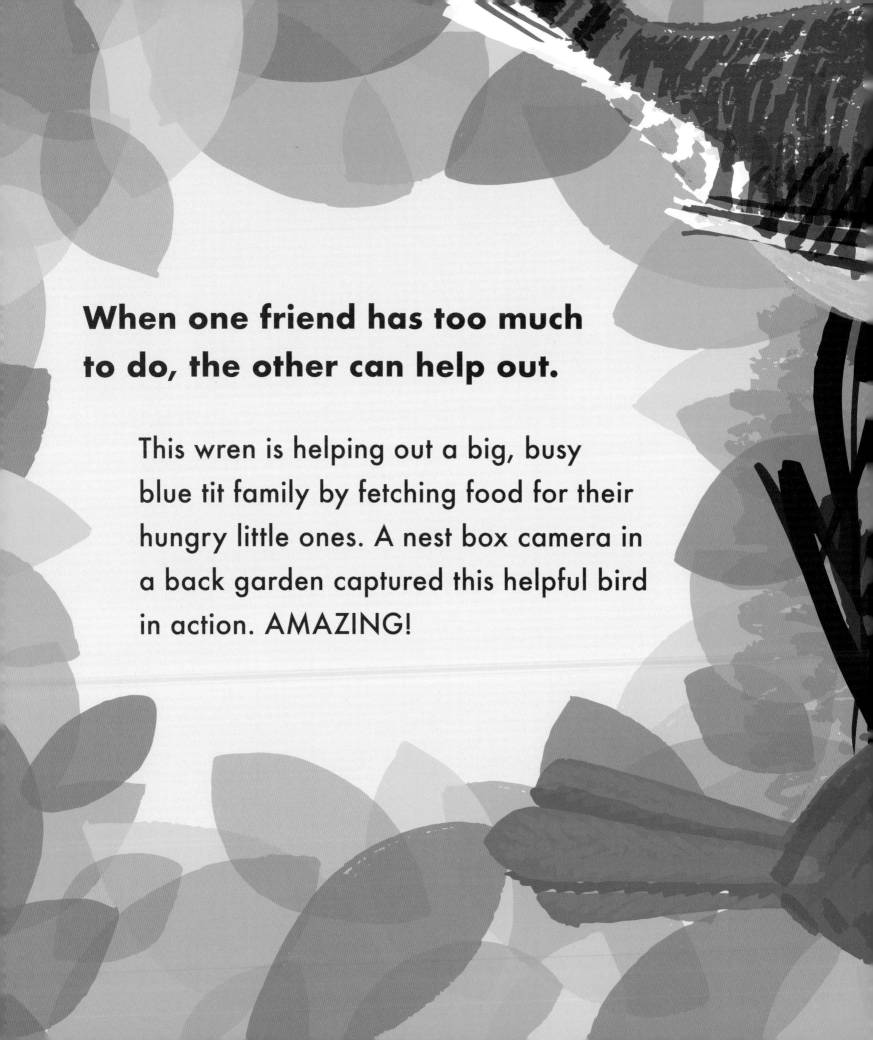

**When one friend has too much to do, the other can help out.**

This wren is helping out a big, busy blue tit family by fetching food for their hungry little ones. A nest box camera in a back garden captured this helpful bird in action. AMAZING!

**Playing together is what some friends do best.**

Some humpback whales and bottlenose dolphins like to play together, splashing about and having fun!

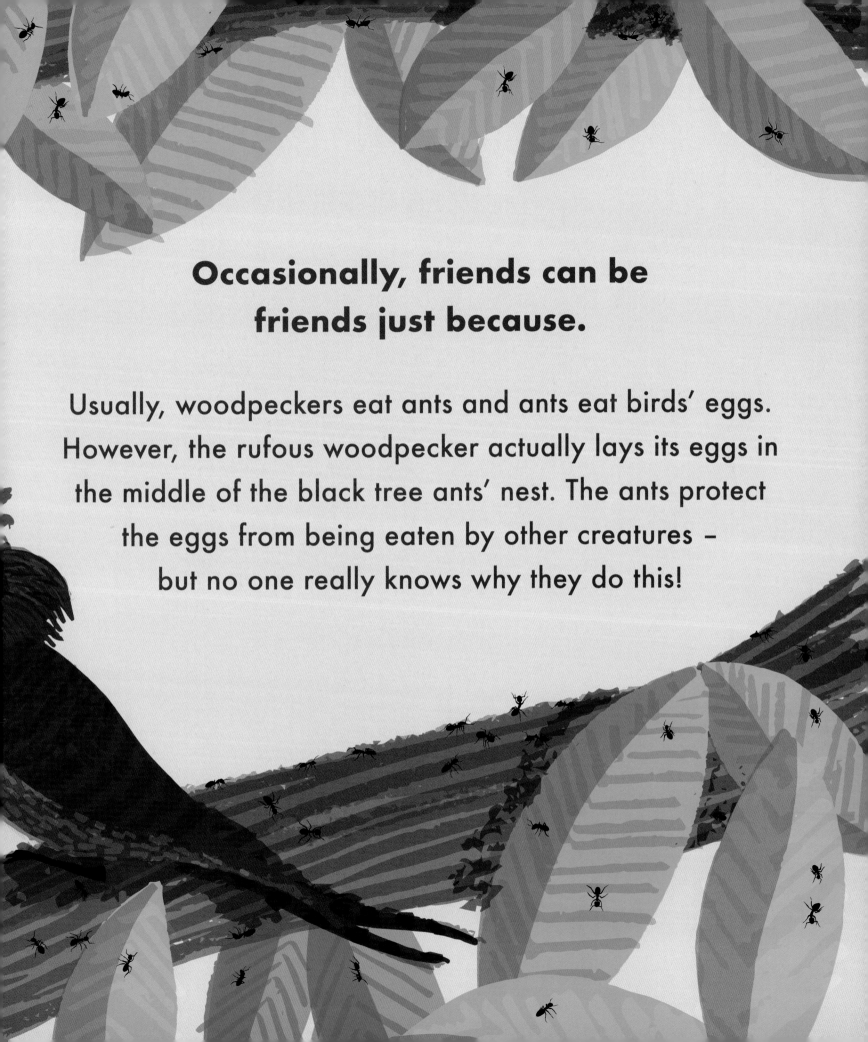

## Occasionally, friends can be friends just because.

Usually, woodpeckers eat ants and ants eat birds' eggs. However, the rufous woodpecker actually lays its eggs in the middle of the black tree ants' nest. The ants protect the eggs from being eaten by other creatures – but no one really knows why they do this!

**Friends trust each other.**

A brave remora fish swims straight into
the jaws of a lemon shark, even though it
could get eaten in a single gulp! However,
instead of eating it, the shark lets the fish clean its
teeth and the fish gets a free meal. MMMMMM!

# You're never lonely if you have friends.

Gertjie the orphaned rhino was rescued, but was very, very lonely in his new home. With no other rhinos to make friends with, Hoedspruit Endangered Species Centre in South Africa paired Gertjie up with Lammie the lamb. They quickly became the best of friends, having fun together all the time!

Yes, there are so many kinds of friendships and each one of them is special . . .

. . . in its own unique way.

# Now you've met each animal, let's find out a little more about them . . .

**Black tree ants** live in India and Sri Lanka. Like most ants they work as a team – building their nest, finding food and protecting their queen.

**Blue tits** usually nest in trees and bird boxes, but they have been known to nest in lamp posts and letter boxes.

**Bottlenose dolphins** communicate with each other by making clicking noises, and can make up to 1,000 clicks per second!

**Chital deer** young have white spots. Unlike other species of deer the spots don't disappear when they become adults.

**Grey langur monkeys** are often found in cities living close to humans. In India, some of these monkeys are trained by humans to scare off other wild animals that might cause mischief.

**Hermit crabs** move shells as they become bigger. When a new shell is spotted, the crabs form a queue from biggest to smallest. The largest crab moves into the new shell and then passes its old shell to the next crab. This continues down the line until they all have a new shell.

**Hippopotamuses** spend a lot of time in the water (they can hold their breath for up to seven minutes), but they can't actually swim! Instead they run along the bottom of the river.

**Humpback whales** have a ginormous tail fin, which is called a fluke. They use it to propel themselves completely out of the water.

**Lambs** are baby sheep. If a sheep rolls onto its back then it can't get back up again. It has to be helped to roll over.

**Lemon sharks** are actually gentle and non-aggressive. They have magnetic sensors in their nose, which means they have a super sense of smell that can detect scents several hundred metres away.

**Ostriches** are the world's largest bird and have the largest eyes of any land animal (up to 5cm in diameter). They also have three stomachs!

**Oxpecker birds** feed exclusively off large mammals. They mainly feast on ticks and parasites, but they have been known to snack on earwax and dandruff too. YUM!

**Remora fish** can be up to 1m long. They attach themselves to sharks using a giant sucker on the top of their heads.

**Rhinoceros** poo has its own distinct and unique scent. Male rhinos use poo to mark out their territory and communicate with other rhinos.

**Rufous woodpeckers** chat by making a nasal sound of 'kweep, kweep, kweep'. Have a go!

**Sea anemones** can be as small as 2cm or as big as 1m. There are more than 1,000 different types of anemones and they come in all the colours of the rainbow.

**Wrens** are small but have mighty voices. In fact, in proportion to their size, they are the loudest British song bird of them all!

**Zebras** each have a unique pattern of stripes, which helps them recognize each other.